fast fun& easy

FABRIC KNITTING

College of the Ouachitas

Cyndy Lyle Rymer

C&T PUBLISHING

Publisher: Amy Marson

Editorial Director: Gailen Runge

Acquisitions Editor: Jan Grigsby

Editor: Lynn Koolish

Technical Editors: Sara Kate MacFarland, Carolyn Aune

Copyeditor/Proofreader: Wordfirm

Cover Designer: Christina Jarumay

Page Layout Artist: Kirstie L. McCormick

Production Assistant: Matt Allen

Photography: Diane Pedersen and Luke Mulks

Published by C&T Publishing, Inc., P.O. Box 1456, Lafayette, CA 94549

Library of Congress Cataloging-in-Publication Data

Rymer, Cyndy Lyle,

   Fast, fun & easy fabric knitting / Cyndy Lyle Rymer.

      p. cm.

   ISBN 1-57120-303-6 (paper trade)

   1. Knitting–Patterns. 2. Textile fabrics. I. Title: Fast, fun, and easy fabric knitting. II. Title.

TT820.R96 2005

   746.43'2–dc22

2004024710

Printed in China

10 9 8 7 6 5 4 3 2 1

Dedication

As always, to John, ever supportive and wonderful; and to Kevin, Zack, and Zana—it's so great watching you unfold and grow! Keep the faith. And to Mom, thanks for your confidence and love.

Acknowledgments

First and foremost, to everyone at C&T Publishing for their continued support and enthusiasm, especially Lynn Koolish, Sara MacFarland, Diane Pedersen, and Luke Mulks. I couldn't ask for better teammates and cheerleaders!

To Janene, Iona, Pat, and Diane at Fashion Knit; and to Catherine Comyns and Jennifer Rounds for their fabulous coaching.

Contents

Knitting With Fabric: Why Not?

All it took to get me hooked on knitting was venturing into a brand-new yarn shop that just happened to open next to a local quilt store. Who could resist all that color and texture so neatly stacked in the bins? I bought some needles and yarn and found another happy place. The tranquility of knitting is a form of therapy for me, just as hand quilting is. Knitting is also portable! No more wasted time waiting in doctors' offices, and now I actually look forward to longer car trips.

I experimented with a few different yarns and had a great time making some simple knitted scarves. One day I had one of those "What if?" moments that got me started on this new journey. What if I cut some of my fabric into strips and tried knitting with them? I found that not only was it possible, but it was also just as addictive as knitting with yarn, and the results were *very* interesting.

For my initial attempts, I cut ½″ strips of fabric from my growing batik collection and started knitting the *Sunset Scarf* (see page 27). I approached it very spontaneously, cutting strips as I needed them. Fun!

What I really liked about the process was that I could still use fabric, my favorite medium. I started by looking through my fabric collection in an effort to use up odd-size pieces in my stash. Then I started buying yardage so my projects would be more consistent in color. The next step was to combine fabric strips with some of the wonderful novelty yarns. The result: the best of both worlds.

It's easy to get started. Try different kinds of fabric and different needle sizes and see what you like. See pages 6–7 for a list of fabrics that work well, including samples of what the fabric looks like when it's knitted. Silk is especially wonderful, even more so when you find it on sale!

New to knitting? For a small project to get you started make the cell phone holder on page 33.

All of the projects are easy to make and should take from a few hours for the smaller projects, to less than a weekend for the bigger ones.

getting started

Knitting with fabric strips will take you into a whole new world. The texture and dimension are great!

Fabrics

cotton

Many cotton fabrics are suitable for stripping and then knitting. Batiks and hand-dyed fabrics work especially well for knitting because both sides of the fabric are consistently beautiful. Commercial prints work well, but the "wrong" side of the fabric is often much lighter than the right side, and sometimes it's even white. When you go fabric shopping, check both sides of the fabric before you buy. One way to control the contrast between the right and wrong side of a fabric is to paint the wrong side.

Tightly woven fabrics, such as pima cottons, are good candidates because they tend to fray less. But, then again, you may like the look of the dangling threads that result when you cut strips with a regular rotary blade (see page 11). The dangling threads add a great texture that's similar to the eyelash yarn that is so popular right now. If you prefer a cleaner look, try cutting the strips with a rotary cutter with a pinking blade (see page 11).

Plaids are fun to play with (see the *Plaid and Silver Shawl* on page 43). Try polka dots—the *All-Occasion Bag* (see page 36) was made with a subtle polka dot. Larger-scale polka dots are fun to knit with as well.

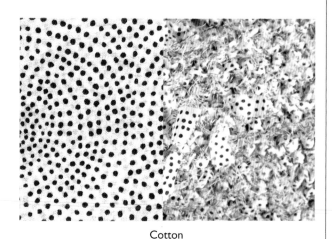

Cotton

flannel

Flannel's soft texture makes it a delight to work with, and the end results are just as cozy as (well, maybe cozier than) any flannel project. Because it is heavier and denser, flannel works well for projects like tote bags, placemats, table runners, pillows, and even slippers. Try working with larger needles, size 11 and up (see page 8 for needles). Also, be aware that many flannels are white on the wrong side. Be sure to prewash flannel, and use a pinking blade to control raveling. Take a look at *Cozy Comfort Flannel Pillow* (see page 44) and *A Charmed Christmas Stocking* (see page 46).

Flannel

easy!

Flannel loves to leave trails of fibers all over you and your surroundings. Get rid of the "confetti" by putting the finished flannel piece in the dryer set to air fluff (no heat) to tumble away some of the loose ends.

rayon

Rayon is another good candidate for fabric knitting. It's soft and drapey. There are many rayon prints, including batiks, which knit up beautifully. You can even recycle rayon garments (see *Why Not Scarf* on page 31). You may want to cut rayon with a pinking blade to control raveling (see page 11).

Rayon

silk

Silk fabric is sumptuous for knitting. Whether you choose habotai, dupioni, crepe de Chine, or charmeuse, you'll want to use a relatively light-weight silk. Some silks are very slippery and may be a bit more challenging to knit with, but the results are worth it. Take at look at *Go Everywhere Poncho* (see page 42); a commercial tie-dyed silk was just perfect for this project!

Silk ribbon, which is available in most yarn shops, is another alternative for knitting.

Silk (plus eyelash yarn)

Prewashing Fabric

Should you prewash the fabric? It's not necessary, but it does make the fabric softer. If you want to get to the fun part—knitting—as quickly as possible, just grab your rotary cutter and some fabric, and start cutting your strips.

However, definitely prewash flannels before knitting to allow for shrinkage.

Yarn

Who can resist all of the novelty yarns available? As you look through this book, you'll notice how easy it is to combine fabric strips with novelty yarns for a great textural appearance. Just knit, working the two strands as one.

Fabric strips and novelty yarns

Needles and Gauge

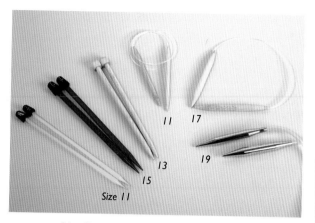

Needles come in various sizes and styles.

needles

There are many needles on the market: long, short, circular; metal, wood, plastic. Shorter ones are great for scarves, and longer needles work well for projects that require more stitches. Circular needles protect projects from the dreaded slip-off-the-needle tragedies, because you can more easily store your project between knitting sessions with the stitches moved to the center of the flexible cable.

easy!

If your circular needle cable refuses to relax and uncurl after you remove it from the packaging, dip it in very hot water until you can straighten the cable.

Try different needles to get the feel and gauge you want. For knitting with fabric, you'll most likely prefer sizes 10½ to 19. These are thicker needles, and they're the easiest to use with fabric strips. You may also find it easier to use plastic needles rather than metal, because the fabric slides more easily. Remember: the bigger the needle size, the larger the stitch, so you'll get fewer stitches per inch.

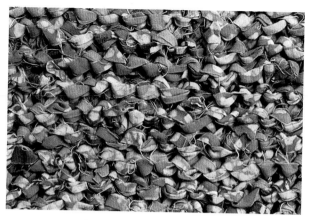

Size 11 needles; 8 stitches = 2

Size 15 needles; 5 stitches = 2

Size 17 needles; 3 stitches = 2

easy!

gauge

Gauge refers to the number of stitches and rows per inch, and a gauge is given for each project. Different fabrics and combinations of yarn and fabric will result in different gauges. Before you start a project, it's a good idea to check your gauge by knitting a 4″ × 4″ square sample with the needles, fabric strips, and yarn you plan to use. You can use a regular ruler or one of the many specialized tools available, such as a knit gauge and needle sizer. The size of the needle you use determines the number of stitches per inch, so you may need to use smaller or larger needles to achieve the correct gauge.

fun!

Press your gauge samples with spray starch, and use them as coasters.

Other Supplies

sewing needles

You'll need a large-eyed needle, such as a tapestry or yarn needle, for sewing together the sides of purses and tote bags. A crochet hook or needle is used to weave in stray ends of fabric strips.

scissors

You'll also want to keep a pair of small scissors with your knitting projects.

point protectors

Point protectors are good to have on hand. These fit on the end of your needles and keep the stitches from falling off in between knitting sessions.

Knitting supplies

preparing fabric

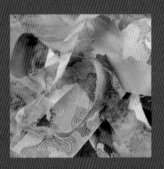

Nothing could be easier than cutting strips to knit with. Grab your rotary cutter and get started!

Cutting

It's easiest to cut strips with a rotary cutter, an acrylic ruler, and a cutting mat. Rotary cutters make quick work of cutting, and you can use either a regular blade or a pinking blade.

Scissors that cut decorative edges, like scallops or waves, are great for freehand cutting.

Cutting supplies

The quickest way to get started knitting is to cut the strips freehand—the strips don't have to be the exact same size. If you prefer, use an acrylic ruler to cut ½″ strips. Cut or tear off the selvage before you cut your strips. If you are working with 40″-wide fabric, fold the fabric lengthwise into fourths so the folded fabric is about 10″ wide and fits easily on your cutting mat. Cut strips about ½″ wide. Slightly less than ½″ also works well, but don't go much narrower than that, or the strips might tear.

Cutting strips with regular rotary blade

fun!

Use a pinking blade on your rotary cutter to add an interesting edge to your strips; this also helps control fraying.

fast!

The June Tailor Shape Cut Plus tool works great for cutting strips, as long as you use a regular blade in the rotary cutter. A yard of fabric can be cut in less than 10 minutes!

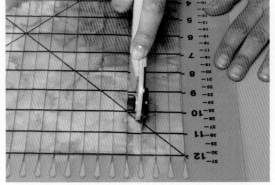

Use June Tailor Shape Cut tool to quickly cut strips.

cutting on the lengthwise grain

For projects that require many strips cut from the same fabric, such as the *Go Everywhere Poncho* (see page 42), fold the fabric in quarters crosswise, and cut strips on the lengthwise grain from the longer yardage.

Joining the Strips

You can join your strips by either tying them together or sewing them together. Each method has several variations.

tying

An easy way to get started is to simply tie the strips together as you go. Try tying 20–30 strips together and rolling them into a ball. You can watch TV, listen to music, or socialize with family and friends while you tie and roll the strips.

Tied strips

easy!

For a smoother look, tie the strips as you need them. This way you can control the location of the knot by planning on which side of the work the knot will fall.

slot knot

This is an especially fast and easy way to anchor strips together.

1. Overlap the ends of 2 strips by about 1″, placing the strip being added on top.

Overlap strips.

2. Fold the strips together in the middle of the 1″ overlap. Make a ¼″ snip in the center of the fold.

Fold in half and snip.

3. Unfold the strips. Pull the other end of the strip being added through from the back and up through the slit created by the snip. Pull the strip through the slit.

Pull other end of strip through from back.

4. Tug gently to form the knot.

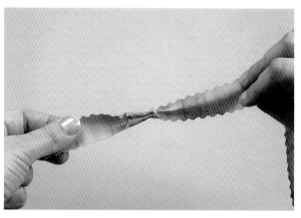

Tug gently.

fast!

One way to avoid knotting or sewing strips together is to open the fabric to a single layer and cut it crosswise, leaving ⅜″ "tabs" on alternate sides.

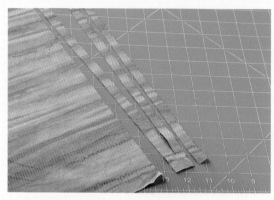

Cut fabric crosswise, stopping ⅜″ from edges.

sewing strips together

If you don't care for the "fabric dangles" that result from tying, you have three choices: weave in the ends; sew all the strips together, end to end, using a small stitch length before you start knitting; or use the slot knot.

Sewing the strips together takes a little longer, but if you like a cleaner look, you may be happier with the results. For the *Some Enchanted Evening Bag* (see page 35), all of the strips were sewn together before they were knitted.

You can sew any lengths of fabric together before you cut them. If you are using fat quarters, it's easiest to cut them in half lengthwise, and then sew them together. Always use a very small stitch length so the seams won't pull apart when you cut the strips.

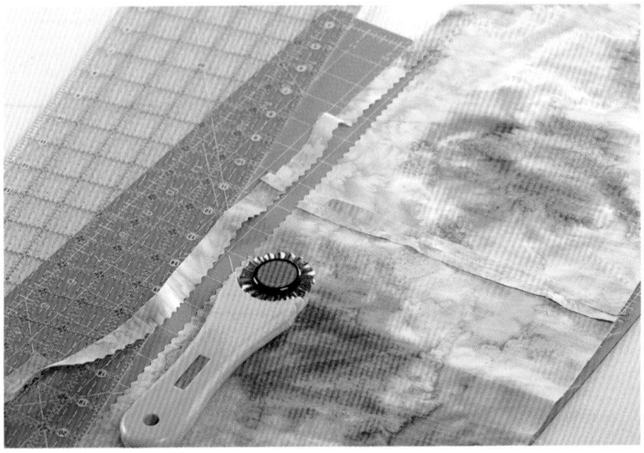

Cut and sew fabric halves together. Cut strips.

easy!

Sew the strips together on the diagonal for a stronger seam.

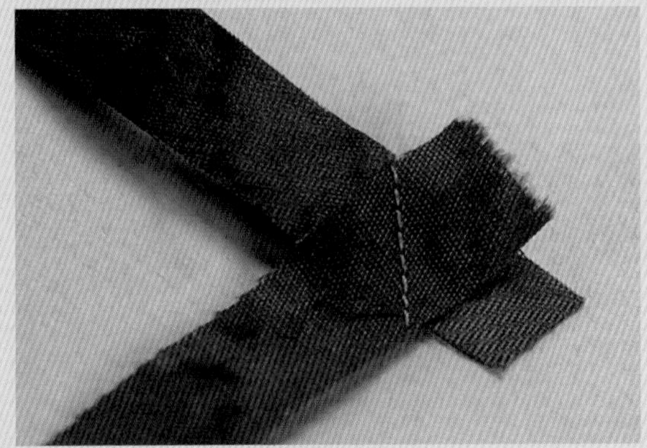

Diagonal seam

continuous bias strips

If you have ever made continuous bias binding, this process will be familiar. You will end up with sewn strips that are much longer than strips cut across the width of the fabric. The prep work will take a little longer, but once the strips are sewn together, they are much longer and are ready to use.

1. Start with a 20″ × 20″ square of fabric. Cut the square in half diagonally so you have 2 triangles.

2. Sew the triangles together, using a small straight stitch and a ¼″ seam allowance. Be sure to sew the edges that are on the straight of grain. Press the seam open.

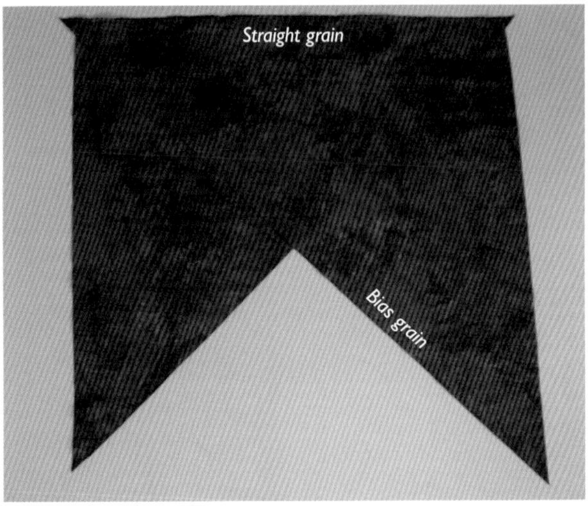

Sew triangles together.

3. Fold the fabric right sides together, forming a tube, and pin. Offset the pinned edges by ½″.

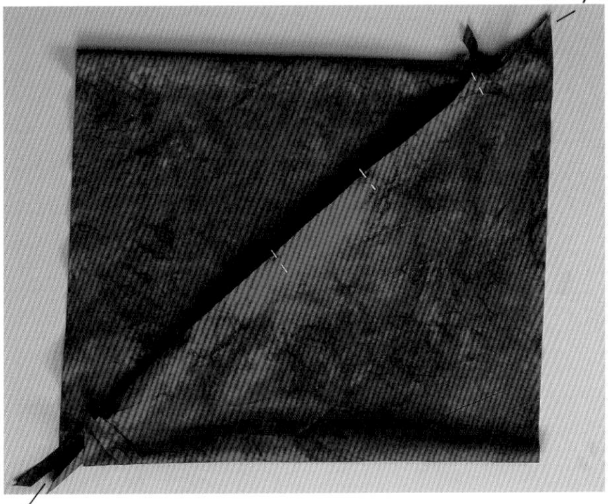

Fold fabric and pin.

4. Sew with a ¼″ seam allowance. Press the seam open.

5. To cut the strips, place the bias tube over your ironing board with a cutting mat under it. Cut until you have worked your way through the entire tube.

Cut.

Storing the Strips

The simplest way to store your strips while you knit is to roll them into a ball, as you would with yarn, and keep the ball in a resealable plastic bag. If you are going to knit with fabric strips and a novelty yarn, it's a good idea to wind the yarn into a separate ball as well (if it is not already in a ball). Most knitting stores will do this for you when you buy the yarn.

easy!

A good way to store balls of fabric strips is to use a recycled baby-wipes box or a large yogurt or cottage cheese container with a hole cut in the lid. Place the strips in the container, and pull the starting end through the hole.

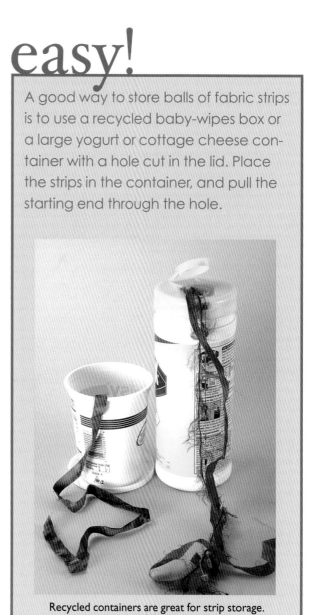

Recycled containers are great for strip storage.

College of the Ouachitas

stitch basics

It's easy to learn knitting basics—just follow the photos. After you learn, you can teach your kids, and they can knit their own projects!

Casting On

Getting the first row of stitches onto your needle—casting on—is the first step. There are several ways to cast on (every knitter has his or her favorite). If you already know how to cast on, feel free to use the method you already use.

start with a slip knot

For both-left handed and right-handed knitters, here's the easiest way to get started.

1. Make a loop by crossing the tail over the working strip (1st loop).

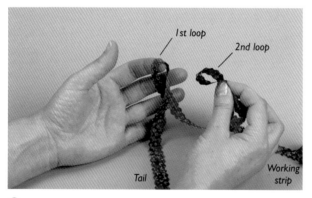

2. Make another loop with the working strip (2nd loop).

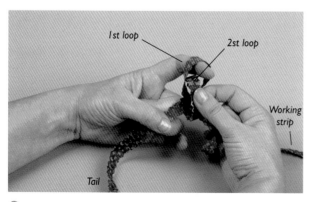

3. Slip the 2nd loop through the 1st loop.

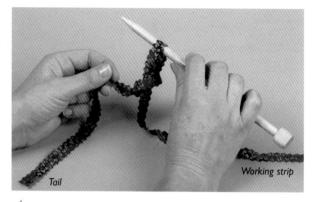

4. Pull the tail to tighten the loop around the needle, but don't pull it too tight.

5. The slip knot is complete and you are ready to cast on.

easy!

If you are left-handed, follow the instructions on the left-hand pages. If you are right-handed, follow the instructions on the right-hand pages.

Left-Handed Casting On

Working strip

Tail

1. Hold the working strip in your right hand

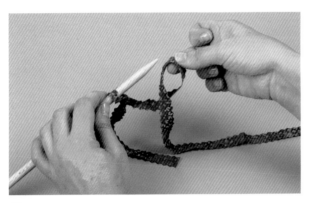

2. Make a loop so the free end of the working strip crosses on top.

3. Place the needle through the loop.

4. Gently pull the working strip to tighten.

5. The first stitch is cast on. Continue in this manner until you have cast on all the stitches for your project. Cast on the stitches loosely to make knitting the first row easier.

easy!

Cast on loosely and knitting the first row is a breeze.

Right-Handed Casting On

Working strip

Tail

1. Hold the working strip in your left hand

2. Make a loop so the free end of the working strip crosses on top.

3. Place the needle through the loop.

4. Gently pull the working strip to tighten.

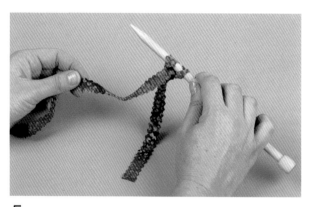

5. The first stitch is cast on. Continue in this manner until you have cast on all the stitches for your project. Cast on the stitches loosely to make knitting the first row easier.

easy!

Cast on loosely and knitting the first row is a breeze.

Left-Handed Knit Stitch

There may be as many ways to knit as there are knitters. Here's the method that I found easiest.

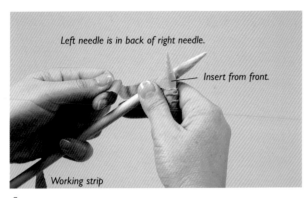

Left needle is in back of right needle.

Insert from front.

Working strip

1. Hold the needle with the cast-on stitches in your right hand; hold the empty needle in your left hand. Slip the tip of the left needle from the front, under and through the front of the loop of the first stitch to the back of the right needle.

2. Use your left hand to wrap the working strip clockwise around the left needle so it falls between the 2 needles.

Bring stitch to front of the right needle.

3. Hold the working strip as you move the left needle down through the stitch, bringing it to the front of the right needle.

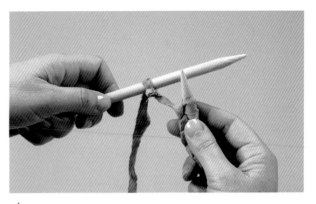

4. Lift the stitch off the right needle with a short forward motion. There is now 1 loop, or stitch, on the left needle.

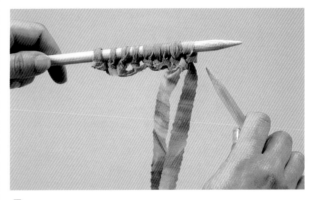

5. Continue knitting until you have finished a row. The stitches have been transferred from 1 needle to the other.

6. Transfer the needle with the completed row to your right hand, and knit the next row. Continue knitting until you have the number of rows called for in the project instructions.

Right-Handed Knit Stitch

There may be as many ways to knit as there are knitters. Here's the method that I found easiest.

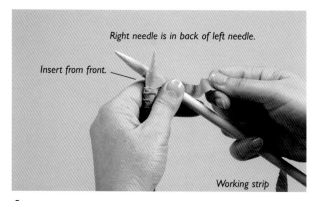

1. Hold the needle with the cast-on stitches in your left hand; hold the empty needle in your right hand. Slip the tip of the right needle from the front, under and through the front of the loop of the first stitch to the back of the left needle.

2. Use your right hand to wrap the working strip counterclockwise around the right needle so it falls between the 2 needles.

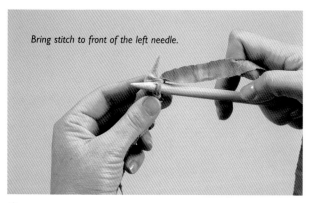

3. Hold the working strip as you move the right needle down through the stitch, bringing it to the front of the left needle.

4. Lift the stitch off the left needle with a short forward motion. There is now 1 loop, or stitch, on the right needle.

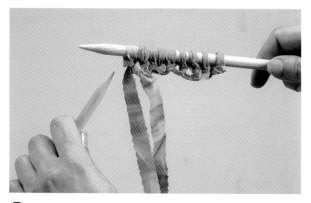

5. Continue knitting until you have finished a row. The stitches have been transferred from 1 needle to the other.

6. Transfer the needle with the completed row to your left hand, and knit the next row. Continue knitting until you have the number of rows called for in the project instructions.

Left-Handed Yarnover/Drop Stitch

Wrap from back to front of left needle.

Working strip

1. Knit a stitch as usual. After you have pulled the stitch onto the left needle, wrap the working strip around the left needle from back to front. Knit another stitch, and wrap the working strip around the needle again. Follow this process of knitting and wrapping to the end of the row. End the row with a knit stitch. This is the yarnover part of the stitch, and it will look like you have twice the number of stitches than you started out with.

2. When you start the next row, knit the first stitch as usual. For the next stitch, pull the yarnover off the needle and let it drop. It will look like a small strip between the other stitches. Knit the next stitch, and let the next yarnover drop. Continue to the end of the row. This is the drop stitch, and it leaves you with the original number of stitches on your needle.

Increasing

Knit 1 stitch, but don't remove it from right needle.

1. Knit a stitch, but don't pull it off the right needle. Slip the point of the left needle behind the right needle and into the back of the same stitch on the right needle.

Slip left needle behind and through back of the same stitch, and knit another stitch.

2. Knit a second stitch from the back of the same loop. Now you can slip both stitches to the left needle.

Decreasing

2 stitches

1. Slip the left needle into the first 2 stitches, and knit them together as a single stitch. You have decreased 1 stitch. Continue knitting, decreasing stitches as required.

Right-Handed Yarnover/Drop Stitch

Wrap from front to back of right needle.

Working strip

1. Knit a stitch as usual. After you have pulled the stitch onto the right needle, wrap the working strip around the right needle from back to front. Knit another stitch, and wrap the working strip around the needle again. Follow this process of knitting and wrapping to the end of the row. End the row with a knit stitch. This is the yarnover part of the stitch, and it will look like you have twice the number of stitches than you started out with.

2. When you start the next row, knit the first stitch as usual. For the next stitch, pull the yarnover off the needle and let it drop. It will look like a small strip between the other stitches. Knit the next stitch, and let the next yarnover drop. Continue to the end of the row. This is the drop stitch, and it leaves you with the original number of stitches on your needle.

Increasing

Knit 1 stitch, but don't remove it from left needle.

1. Knit a stitch, but don't pull it off the left needle. Slip the point of the right needle behind the left needle and into the back of the same stitch on the left needle.

Slip right needle behind and through back of the same stitch, and knit another stitch.

2. Knit a second stitch from the back of the same loop. Now you can slip both of the stitches to the right needle.

Decreasing

2 stitches

1. Slip the right needle into the first 2 stitches, and knit them together as a single stitch. You have

Left-Handed Binding Off

1. Knit the first 2 stitches. Use your fingers or the tip of your right needle to pull the first stitch over the top of the second stitch and off the left needle. You now have 1 stitch remaining on the left needle.

2. Knit another stitch, so you again have 2 stitches on the left needle. Pull the first stitch over the second stitch and off the needle.

3. Continue the process until you have only 1 stitch remaining on the left needle and none on the right.

4. Cut your working strip so there are about 3″ left. Carefully slip the last stitch off the needle, and thread the end of the strip through the loop of the stitch.

5. Pull gently to tighten.

easy!

Keep your binding-off stitches loose for a smooth finish to your project.

Right-Handed Binding Off

1. Knit the first 2 stitches. Use your fingers or the tip of your left needle to pull the first stitch over the top of the second stitch and off the right needle. You now have 1 stitch remaining on the right needle.

2. Knit another stitch, so you again have 2 stitches on the right needle. Pull the first stitch over the second stitch and off the needle.

3. Continue the process until you have only 1 stitch remaining on the right needle and none on the left.

4. Cut your working strip so there are about 3˝ left. Carefully slip the last stitch off the needle, and thread the end of the strip through the loop of the stitch.

5. Pull gently to tighten.

easy!

Keep your binding-off stitches loose for a smooth finish to your project.

Sewing Seams

Projects such as purses and bags need to have a seam or two sewn together. These seams are easy to sew using a large-eyed needle such as a tapestry or yarn needle.

1. Thread the needle with a fabric strip that matches your project.

2. Insert the needle into a loop on one of the pieces to be joined, then insert it into a loop on the other piece to be joined.

Use tapestry needle threaded with fabric strip.

3. Pull the fabric strip through. Take as many stitches as needed to sew the pieces together.

Pull fabric strip through.

4. End by tying a knot. Use a crochet hook to weave the end of the fabric strip back into the knit fabric.

Blocking

Some of the knitted projects may be stretched a bit out of shape when finished. Use blocking to straighten out a knit project.

1. Spray the project with water from a spray bottle.

2. Lay it out on a towel on a flat surface and gently tug into shape. You may need to pull it at both ends to straighten and lengthen it a bit.

3. Use T-pins to hold the project in place, and let it dry overnight. You'll be rewarded with a much straighter project.

You can also put a project sprayed with water in the dryer on low heat until it is just slightly damp, and then block it as described above.

sunset scarf

An incredibly beautiful sunset inspired this colorful scarf. Choose any five colors that you love.

SUNSET SCARF,
Cyndy Rymer, Danville, CA

FINISHED SIZE:
3½" x 52" (without fringe)

What You'll Need

- ☐ 1¾ yards total fabric: 7 quarter-yard cuts in a variety of colors
- ☐ Knitting needles, size 11
- ☐ Large tapestry needle
- ☐ Crochet hook
- ☐ Optional: Yarn or ribbon for fringe

Gauge: 4 stitches = 1″; 5 rows = 3″

How-To's

See pages 11–26 for Preparing Fabrics and Stitch Basics.

1. Cut the fabrics into ½″ strips. Sew or tie the strips of each color together into long strips, and roll into balls. (If you have fat quarters, see pages 13–14 for cutting fat quarters in half and sewing to create longer strips.)

2. Start by casting on 14 stitches.

3. Knit about 4 rows with each color, or as many rows as desired.

4. Knit 86 rows, or until your scarf measures approximately 52″.

5. Bind off.

6. Add fringe by folding 14″-long strips of fabric and yarn or ribbon in half. Pull 2″ of the folded end of the strip through the bottom of every second stitch. Use your crochet hook as necessary to open the stitch and pull the strip through. Pass the ends of the strips through the loop created. Gently tug to create a knot.

Insert folded fringe strips.

Pass strips through loop.

fun!

Tie or sew beads onto the ends of the strips for a decorative touch. The beads will also add a little weight to the fringe.

rainbow sorbet
scarf

Gradated, hand-dyed fabrics are perfect for this scarf; a multicolored mohair yarn with metallic threads adds just the right amount of sparkle.

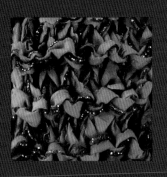

RAINBOW SORBET SCARF,
Cyndy Rymer, Danville, CA

FINISHED SIZE: $2\frac{3}{4}" \times 82\frac{1}{2}"$

What You'll Need

- ☐ 16 gradated fat quarters
- ☐ Mohair/metallic yarn
- ☐ Knitting needles, size 19
- ☐ Large tapestry needle

How-To's

See pages 11–26 for Preparing Fabrics and Stitch Basics.

1. See pages 13–14 for cutting fat quarters in half and sewing to create longer strips. Cut each fat quarter into strips. Sew or tie the strips of each color together into a strip, and roll into balls.

2. Start by casting on 7 stitches. If you are using yarn with your fabric, cast on and knit the fabric strip and yarn as 1 strand.

3. Change colors randomly at the beginning of a row by tying or hand (or machine) stitching the next color onto the end of the last strip.

4. Knit 110 rows or until your scarf measures approximately 70″.

5. Bind off.

6. Add fringe by folding 14″-long strips of fabric and yarn or ribbon (optional) in half. Pull 2″ of the folded end of the strip through the bottom of every second stitch. Use your crochet hook as necessary to open the stitch and pull the strip through. Pass the ends of the strips through the loop created. Gently tug to create a knot. (See page 28.)

easy!

Keep a needle and matching sewing thread on hand. Sometimes the strips that have been sewn together will pull apart while you are knitting. Don't panic. Just stitch them back together by hand with a needle and thread.

fun!

Plan your color order, and pick a color to use as the midpoint. Knit the colors in order to the midpoint, and then reverse the color order for the second half of the scarf.

A. If you love the color purple, or are a member of the Red Hat Society, this is the scarf for you! Add some beads throughout for a bit of glitz and glam.

B. Here's a scarf made from a recycled 8-gore rayon skirt. The strips were cut in a continuous spiral, starting at the bottom of the skirt.

C. Hand-dyed silk ribbon makes a sumptuous scarf. Yarnover/dropped stitches were used just at the ends of the scarf.

Purple Passion Scarf, Cyndy Rymer, Danville, CA

Why Not Scarf, Lynn Koolish, Berkeley, CA

simple
accessories

Here are *fast* accessories you can make for yourself or give as gifts. They are great projects to start with. Measure your cell phone or eyeglasses first—you may have to adjust the size.

SIMPLE ACCESSORIES,
Cyndy Rymer, Danville, CA

FINISHED SIZE: 4″ x 4″ closed

FINISHED SIZE: 3″ x 6″ closed

FINISHED SIZE: 3″ x 5″ closed

What You'll Need

- ☐ ⅓ yard of fabric
- ☐ Knitting needles, size 11 for cell phone holder or eyeglass case; size 13 for pocket organizer (such as a Palm Pilot) case
- ☐ Large tapestry needle
- ☐ Optional: Novelty yarn
- ☐ Optional: Flannel or felt scraps for eyeglass case liner

- ☐ Optional: Charms, bracelet clasp, beads, wine charm loop, 26-gauge craft wire, needle-nose pliers
- ☐ Optional: Small square of hook-and-loop tape for fastener on cases with flaps

Gauge: 3 stitches = 1″; 3 rows = 1″

How-To's

See pages 11–26 for Preparing Fabrics and Stitch Basics.

cell phone case

1. Cut the fabric into ¼″ strips. Sew or tie them together into a long strip, and roll into a ball.

2. Start by casting on 10 stitches. If you are using a novelty yarn with your fabric, cast on and knit the fabric strip and novelty yarn as 1 strand.

3. Knit 33 rows or until it measures approximately 10″ long.

4. Bind off.

5. Fold the front up so the case is 4″ long with a 2″ flap that folds over from the back. Stitch the sides together, leaving the flap free. (See page 26.)

Sew a special charm in the center of the foldover flap.

eyeglass case

1. Cut the fabric into ¼″ strips. Sew or tie them together into a long strip, and roll into a ball.

2. Start by casting on 10 stitches. If you are using a novelty yarn along with your fabric, cast on and knit the fabric strip and novelty yarn as 1 strand.

3. Knit 35 rows or until it measures approximately 13″ long.

4. For the next row, decrease by knitting together 2 stitches at the beginning and end of the row.

5. Repeat Step 4 until you have 1 stitch remaining on your needle.

6. Cut the remaining strip to a length of 3″. Slip the strip through the last stitch and tighten.

7. Leaving the flap free, fold the remaining length in half, and sew the sides together to form a 6″ long case. (See page 26.)

8. Fold the leftover strip at the end of the flap in half. Slip the folded strip through a bracelet clasp ring. Fold again to the back of the flap, and stitch in place.

9. Use craft wire to attach beads to the bracelet clasp.

easy!

pocket organizer case

1. Cut the fabric into ¼″ strips. Sew or tie them together into a long strip, and roll into a ball.

2. Start by casting on 12 stitches. If you are using a novelty yarn with your fabric, cast on and knit the fabric strip and novelty yarn as 1 strand.

3. Knit 25 rows or until it measures approximately 9″ long.

4. For the next row, decrease by knitting together 2 stitches at the beginning and end of the row.

5. Repeat Step 4 until you have 1 stitch remaining on your needle.

6. Fold the front up 4″. Stitch the sides together. (See page 26.)

Variations

A. Knit a smaller cell phone case for an attractive—and hard to misplace—home for your flip phone.

B. Stitch a square of hook-and-loop tape inside the flap, and add a decorative button on the front. Thread small pieces of craft wire through stitches on the bottom of the case, and add beads. Twist the ends of the wire around your tapestry needle so the beads stay put.

C. Combine strips of metallic fabric and eyelash yarn to make a fun eyeglass case.

CELL PHONE AND EYEGLASS CASES
Cyndy Rymer, Danville, CA

some enchanted evening bag

No special occasion is needed to enjoy this glitzy little evening bag. It's an ideal gift idea for your best friend, or make it up in red and green or blue and silver for winter holidays.

SOME ENCHANTED EVENING BAG,
Cyndy Rymer, Danville, CA

FINISHED SIZE: 8˝ × 6½˝

What You'll Need

- 1¾ yards black and gold cotton/metallic fabric
- 2 different gold metallic yarns, including 1 skein of gold eyelash for flap
- 1 yard black and gold cording for strap
- Black quilting or topstitching thread (for sewing on cording)
- Knitting needles, size 10½
- Large tapestry needle
- Optional: ½″ black hook-and-loop squares for closure
- Optional: Gold charm or button for tip of flap

Gauge: 8 stitches = 2″; 6 rows = 2″

How-To's

See pages 11–26 for Preparing Fabrics and Stitch Basics.

bag

1. Cut the fabric into ½″ strips. Sew or tie them together into a long strip, and roll into a ball.

2. Start by casting on 30 stitches with the fabric strip and gold metallic yarn.

3. Knit 39 rows or until it measures approximately 13″ long.

4. Tie the eyelash yarn onto the other gold metallic yarn.

5. Knit 1 full row with all 3 fibers the black/gold strips, gold metallic yarn, and gold metallic eyelash.

6. For the next row, decrease by knitting together 2 stitches at the beginning and end of the row.

7. Decrease by 1 stitch at the beginning and end of the remaining rows until there is 1 stitch left. Thread the tail through the loop, tug gently, and trim the tail. Weave about 1½″ of the tail into the middle of the flap.

8. Fold the front up so the bag measures 6½″ deep. Sew the sides of the bag together with fabric strips. (See page 26.)

strap

1. Sew the cording onto the sides on the inside of the bag, using quilting or topstitching thread and a tapestry needle.

2. Sew 1 part of the hook-and-loop tape onto the envelope flap, and sew the other half onto the front of the bag.

Variation

The *All-Occasion Bag* is a variation of the evening bag—instead of the pointed envelope flap, knit a rectangular flap with a feathery yarn instead of fabric.

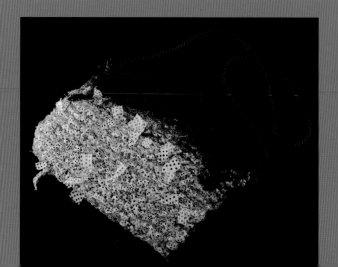

All-Occasion Bag, Cyndy Rymer, Danville, CA

calypso bag

This adaptable little bag, which is jazzed up with purchased handles, is a perfect purse that can go anywhere. Picture it in red, white, and blue for Fourth of July fun.

CALYPSO BAG,
Cyndy Rymer, Danville, CA

FINISHED SIZE: 8″ × 10″ plus handle

What You'll Need

- ☐ 1¼ yards fuchsia fabric
- ☐ ⅓ yard white or peach fabric
- ☐ ⅓ yard dark peach fabric
- ☐ Knitting needles, size 15
- ☐ Large tapestry needle

- ☐ Purchased bamboo handles
- ☐ Optional: ⅓ yard fabric for lining
- ☐ Optional: Perle cotton or embroidery floss for sewing lining into bag

Gauge: 5 stitches = 2″; 5 rows = 2″

How-To's

See pages 11–26 for Preparing Fabrics and Stitch Basics.

bag

1. Cut the fabrics into ½″ strips. Sew or tie the fuchsia strips together and roll into a ball; this is the color you will use the most.

2. Start by casting on 19 stitches with fuchsia.

3. Knit 3 rows.

4. Tie on a white/peach strip. For the next row, increase 1 stitch at the beginning and end of the row.

5. Tie on a dark peach strip. For the next row, increase 1 stitch at the beginning and end of the row. Knit 1 more row.

6. Continue by tying on and knitting: 1 row of white/peach, 2 rows of dark peach, 12 row of fuchsia, 3 rows of dark peach, 12 rows of fuchsia, 2 rows of dark peach, and 1 row of white/peach.

7. Tie on a dark peach strip. Knit 1 row. For the next row, decrease by knitting together 2 stitches at the beginning and end of the row.

8. Tie on a white/peach strip. For the next row, decrease by knitting together 2 stitches at the beginning and end of the row.

9. Tie on a fuchsia strip. Knit 3 rows.

10. Bind off.

optional lining

1. Cut a rectangle 8½″ × 20″.

2. Create a finished hem on the shorter ends by folding and pressing the ends under by ½″ and then a second ½″. Topstitch.

3. Fold the lining in half vertically with right sides together. Stitch sides together. Slip lining into bag.

4. With wrong sides out, tack the lining to a side and to a top edge of the bag. Fold the knitted bag in half, and carefully sew the lining to the second side of the bag about ½″ from the edge of the bag. Sew the lining to the other top edge of the bag.

5. Use a fuchsia fabric strip and the tapestry needle to sew the sides of the bag together. (See page 26.)

6. To attach the bag to the handles, use fuchsia strips and the tapestry needle to wrap the strip around the handles and through the top row of the knitted bag.

Use strips to attach the bag to the handles.

big tote

What a fun tote for the beach or for visits to the farmers' market! Add a lining for a more durable bag. Add a pocket on the lining, and you have a place to stash keys, cash, and whatever else you need to find quickly.

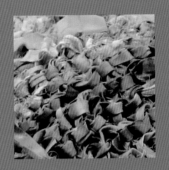

BIG TOTE, Cyndy Rymer, Danville, CA

FINISHED SIZE: 15˝ × 14˝ plus strap

What You'll Need

- [ ] 3 yards total fabric: A variety of ¼-yard cuts of fabric (10–12) in 1 color family
- [ ] Knitting needles, size 17 for bag, size 11 for strap
- [ ] Large tapestry needle
- [ ] Beads for braided closure
- [ ] Optional: ½ yard of fabric for lining
- [ ] Optional: Perle cotton or embroidery floss for sewing lining onto bag

Gauge: 7 stitches = 3″; 5 rows = 2″

How-To's

See pages 11–26 for Preparing Fabrics and Stitch Basics.

tote

1. Cut the fabrics into ½″ strips. There is no need to roll the strips into a ball, because you will change colors randomly at the ends of rows by tying in new colors.

2. Start by casting on 35 stitches.

3. Knit about 6 rows with each color, or as many rows as desired.

4. Knit 70 rows or until it measures approximately 14″ long.

5. Bind off.

6. Fold the bag in half **lengthwise**. If you plan to line the bag, go to Step 1 below. Stitch the side and bottom seams together. (See page 26.)

optional lining

1. Cut a rectangle 14½″ × 29″.

2. Create a finished hem by folding and pressing the top and bottom edges under by ½″ and then a second ½″. Topstitch.

3. Fold the lining in half vertically.

4. For an optional interior pocket, cut a rectangle 6″ × 7″. Fold under ½″ on the top and bottom, and then the sides, for a clean edge. Stitch around all sides; use a built-in embroidery stitch to add a decorative detail, if desired.

easy!

Before sewing the pocket to the lining, add hook-and-loop tape to the pocket and lining for more security.

5. Center the pocket on the right side of a side of the lining. Pin and stitch in place.

6. Stitch the sides of the lining with right sides together. Press. Do not turn right side out.

7. Slip the lining into the bag. Using the tapestry needle and perle cotton, sew along the top edge to of the bag. Stitch the bottom of the lining to the knitted bag with a loose running stitch between the knitted stitches across the width of the bag.

strap

1. Switch to size 11 needles for a tighter stitch—the strap won't stretch out as much if you use smaller needles.

2. Cast on 7 stitches.

3. Knit. When it measures approximately 30″, test the length for a comfortable fit, and then keep knitting until you reach the right length for you. Tie the strap to bag.

braided closure with beads (optional)

1. Fold 3 leftover strips of fabric in half, and tie them together in the center for a total of 6 strands.

2. Tape or tie the strips to a solid surface. Use 2 strips for each strand of the braid, and braid the strands together until you have a strip about 8″ long. Tie the braid together into 1 big knot.

3. Make a knot in each strip about 2″ from the end of the strip.

4. Roll the ends of the strips so they are narrow enough to travel through a large-hole bead. Thread the strip through a bead, and make a knot to hold the bead in place.

Braiding the closure

easy!

Make this a drawstring bag by weaving a length of ribbon through the top of the bag. Add decorative beads or charms to add weight to the end of the ribbon drawstring.

Variation

Make a tiny tote for your passport and travel essentials. You can wear it under your jacket for greater security.

go everywhere
poncho

Larger needles are great to work with, especially when you knit with silk! This quick-to-knit poncho features yarnover/dropped stitches that create a lacy look. Give it some extra color by knitting with eyelash yarn.

GO EVERYWHERE PONCHO,
Cyndy Rymer, Danville, CA

FINISHED SIZE: completed rectangle approximately 42˝ × 18˝

FINISHED PONCHO: 21˝ × 18˝

What You'll Need

- ☐ 6½ yards green-yellow silk fabric
- ☐ Knitting needles, size 19
- ☐ Large tapestry needle
- ☐ Optional: Eyelash yarn

Gauge: 6 stitches = 4″; 4 rows = 4″

How-To's

See pages 11–26 for Preparing Fabrics and Stitch Basics.

1. Keep the fabric folded as it came off the bolt, and carefully fold the fabric crosswise into quarters. Trim the selvages. Cut ½″ strips on the lengthwise grain. This folding process makes cutting very quick.

2. Start by casting on 32 stitches. If you are using yarn with your fabric, cast on and knit the fabric strip and yarn as 1 strand.

3. Knit 5 rows.

4. Knit 1 stitch, yarnover twice, then knit another stitch, and yarnover twice again. Continue in this manner across the row to the last stitch. Knit the last stitch. Knit the next row, dropping the stitches created with the yarnovers and knitting only the stitches knitted in the previous row.

5. Knit 2 rows.

6. Repeat Steps 4–5 until the rectangle measures approximately 42″. Add more rows for a larger poncho.

7. Bind off.

8. Fold the rectangle in half so the short edges meet. Use a tapestry needle and strips of silk to sew a closing seam along one of the long sides of the rectangle to within 10″ or so of the fold, leaving an opening wide enough to slip the poncho over your head.

fun!

Add fringe to one side of the poncho. For an interesting touch, add beaded tassels to the points of the poncho.

Variation

A combination of knitted stitches and yarnover/dropped stitches was used to create this shawl. Lightweight plaid fabric and silver, fuzzy yarn make it perfect to wear with everything!

Plaid and Silver Shawl, Cyndy Rymer, Danville, CA

cozy comfort
flannel pillow

Give someone you love a comfy place to lay their head at the end of a long day. Have fun choosing different colors for the squares!

COZY COMFORT FLANNEL PILLOW,
Cyndy Rymer, Danville, CA

FINISHED SIZE: 16″ × 16″

What You'll Need

- ☐ 3–4 yards each of 2 contrasting or coordinating plaid flannels (54″-wide fabric was used for the pillow shown; if you use 40″-wide fabric, buy 4–5 yards.)
- ☐ Knitting needles, size 15
- ☐ Large tapestry needle
- ☐ Buttonhole thread
- ☐ 16″ × 16″ pillow form
- ☐ 2 large buttons

Gauge: 5 stitches = 2″; 6 rows = 3″

How-To's

See pages 11–26 for Preparing Fabrics and Stitch Basics.

squares for pillow front

1. Cut the fabrics into ½″ strips. Sew or tie them together into a long strip, and roll into a ball.

2. Cast on 18 stitches, using the first color strip.

3. Knit 15 rows or until square measures 7½″. Bind off.

4. Make 1 more square with the first color, and then make 2 squares with the second color.

5. Stitch the 4 squares together with extra fabric strips to form a square pillow front.

Stitch squares together.

pillow back

1. Cast on 30 stitches.

2. Knit 25 rows or until it measures 15½″. Bind off.

assembly

1. Use extra fabric strips to stitch the pillow front to the pillow back on the sides and bottom, leaving the top open.

2. Insert the pillow form. Pull the front and back, stretching it to fit the form. Stitch the top closed with extra fabric strips. The pillow covering will be a tight fit.

3. Sew through the pillow to attach the front and back buttons.

Variation

A bright, multicolored plaid shot through with metallic threads was used to make this fun 14″ x 14″ pillow. The front knits up in just 3 hours! Use one piece of fabric for the back. What could be easier?

PASTEL PILLOW,
Cyndy Rymer, Danville, CA

a charmed christmas stocking

Make an oversized Christmas stocking large enough to hold lots of goodies (or a year's supply of coal). Embellish with beads, charms, buttons, or little Christmas ornaments.

A CHARMED CHRISTMAS STOCKING,
Gael Betts, Walnut Creek, CA

FINISHED SIZE: 7˝ × 18˝ (with the cuff folded over)

What You'll Need

- □ 2½ yards red flannel
- □ ¾ yard white flannel
- □ 1 skein white eyelash yarn
- □ Knitting needles, size 17
- □ Large tapestry needle
- □ Crochet hook
- □ Optional: Beads

Gauge: 3 stitches = 1¾"; 3 rows = 1¾"

How-To's

See pages 11–26 for Preparing Fabrics and Stitch Basics.

1. Cut the red flannel into ½" strips. Sew or tie them together into a long strip, and roll into a ball.

2. Cut the white flannel into ½" strips.

stocking front

1. Start by casting on 15 stitches.

2. Knit 1 row.

3. Increase at the beginning and end of each row for the next 4 rows until you have 23 stitches on the needle.

4. Knit until the foot of the stocking measures 4½" high.

5. On the next row, bind off 2 stitches from the toe side of the stocking. Knit the remaining 21 stitches to the end of the row.

6. Repeat binding off 2 stitches on the toe of the stocking and knitting until there are 13 stitches left on the needle.

7. Knit until the top of the stocking is 12" long.

8. To make the cuff, trim the remaining red strip so it's about 3" long. Tie the start of the white flannel to the red strip. Hold strips of white flannel and white eyelash yarn together as a unit. Knit rows until the cuff is about 5", or longer if you prefer. Bind off.

stocking back

Repeat Steps 1–8 for the back of the stocking.

finishing

1. Sew the front and back together. (see page 26). Use red strips for the body of the stocking and white strips for the cuff.

fun!

The tiny strips that result from tying the strips together are a perfect place to sew charms.

Variation

Knit up some extra-warm booties as a great and easy gift. The fabric strips are doubled and used as one strand to make these extra toasty.

Happy Holiday Booties, Gael Betts, Walnut Creek, CA

About the Author

Cyndy Lyle Rymer, a newcomer to knitting, is an editor at C&T Publishing. Her first love is quilting, but the beautiful yarns available today turned her head when a new knitting store, Fashion Knit, opened in nearby Walnut Creek, California. She soon discovered that her favorite medium—fabric—could also be used to knit. Now she is faced with a daily dilemma: deciding whether to knit or quilt.

Danville, California, is home to Cyndy's living-room-turned-studio. She shares the other rooms of her house with husband, John, and children, Kevin, Zack, and Zana, and with wonderful Arlo, a Shetland sheepdog who is the center of the family's universe. Her mom, Marie Lyle, is president of Cyndy's fan club, even though she has no idea where Cyndy's interest in needle arts came from.

Resources

knitting supplies

www.software4knitting.com

www.yarnmarket.com

www.herrschners.com

purse handles

Sunbeltfastener.com

800-642-6587

email: info@sunbeltfastnener.com

june tailor shape cut plus

www.junetailor.com

for more information

Ask for a free catalog:
C&T Publishing, Inc.
P.O. Box 1456
Lafayette, CA 94549
800-284-1114
email: ctinfo@ctpub.com
website: www.ctpub.com

fabric

Cotton Patch Mail Order
3404 Hall Lane
Dept. CTB
Lafayette, CA 94549
800-835-4418
925-283-7883
email: quiltusa@yahoo.com
website: www.quiltusa.com

Note: Because manufacturers keep most fabrics and yarns available for only a short time, fabrics and yarns used in the projects shown may not be currently available.